Customer Experience Culture In Government

Principles, Practices, & Measures

Daryl Covey

Cgov

Community of Practice

August, 2018

DEDICATION

I dedicate this book to the people who strive daily at the front lines of government to deliver the most responsive customer experience possible -- despite the politics, budget issues, bureaucracy, micromanagement, cumbersome regulations, and apathy which are too often obstacles to doing so. As I have interacted with them at all levels of government over the past several decades, they've never failed to impress me with their focus on serving their customer and their embrace of the need to continually improve the customer's experience. From massive virtual federal call centers to the web site keeper at town hall, their devotion to what they do is truly inspiring. I applaud them on behalf of *all of us* for the dedication they bring to what they do *every day*!

Daryl Covey
August, 2018

ACKNOWLEDGEMENTS

Throughout my thirty year quest to foster networking and the exchange of effective practices among those who deliver the services of government, I've been consistently blessed along the way with access to thought leaders. Authors, speakers, institute leaders, and many others from both public and private sectors have readily stepped forward to share their perspectives on delivering a quality experience to our customer. I thank them for their time and genuine interest in enhancing what we do.

Even more so, I thank the government practitioners who have shared their service stories in well over a thousand award nominations as well as countless presentations and personal conversations, each adding focus to the picture of what customer experience culture in our sector really looks like. They are true heroes -- immersed in what they do, yet finding time in the midst of doing it to give back to their professional community.

I also thank all of the distinguished people who have stepped forward over the past eighteen years to serve as judges of our award nominations, as well as those who have partnered with us to present our awards and showcase our winners in their respective conference programs.

Finally, and most of all, I thank my family for their patient understanding while Dad was pursuing his quest. It has meant everything.

CONTENTS

PREFACE

The *customer experience (CX)* paradigm for customer care originated in the private sector. It is rooted in the commercial concept of *"brand image"* which is *the summary impression resulting from all interactions (direct or indirect) with the source of a product or service.* Today, CX is receiving massive attention as the new panacea for public sector service delivery. But in government, absent the glossy professional branding practices of the private sector, the only brand we have to work with is our *culture.* It permeates everything we do and we are known by it! And it's where the successful adoption or improvement of *any* service paradigm in our sector must begin!

Like any other service model born in the private sector, CX will require careful adaptation, insightful implementation, and especially the right supporting culture to be viable for us and our customer. The latter is the ultimate key to success! It has been insightfully defined as, "where management *understands* what both front line employees and customers are *experiencing*." Ironically, this culture has already long existed in disconnected pockets throughout government, but knowledge of just what it is and how it works has not been previously shared in any comprehensive form. Our objective here is to finally and uniquely do so, after thirty years of searching it out across government, in order to help us *all* deliver information and services in the best possible way.

We thank you the reader for your time investment in better government service delivery as you consider what we have to share.

INTRODUCTION

I was educated, interned, and delighted to serve the public as an operational scientist during the first half of my federal career. It was deeply gratifying to protect people and enhance the quality of their lives by applying my education and growing experience! However, as my seniority increased, my career turned toward a more specialized discipline of technology-based operational science in which epic advances began just as I gained proficiency. Little did I know that this new career direction would lead me to a whole new passion in life!

In the late 1980s I was approached by the director of a multi-agency acquisition program to establish a comprehensive help desk for the billion-dollar global network of field systems it would produce. The project was under the Congressional microscope and would need a high level of early success in operations to receive full multi-year funding for deployment. The related technology and science were so new that thousands of people in three federal departments working worldwide would need access to immediate expert assistance to succeed in their respective critical missions. As a famous person at NASA once said, failure in this endeavor was "not an option." Excited about my new specialty, having previous experience in the program, and with the unmitigated enthusiasm of youth, I readily accepted the challenge by essentially saying, "Sure!" "But what's a help desk?" The learning curve which followed would be both massive and fascinating!

I won't bore you with lots of details here, but what grew from that conversation became one of the most recognized contact centers in government. As we filled a wall with awards and blew past recognized industry benchmarks for excellence -- despite the unique complexity of both our mission and customer base -- I pondered what had fundamentally driven this totally unexpected high level of success. As I did so, I kept returning to how we'd had to bootstrap our implementation without a body of knowledge to reference in doing so. And there I found the gold nugget! Absent proven guidance we focused on what we knew best: *ourselves and the people we would be serving.* As for ourselves the focus converged on being comprehensively prepared to immediately resolve complex issues in an empathetic manner -- a very tall order! As for the people we would be serving, after careful consideration, it was the *same answer!* Fortunately, since our initial staffing was drawn from the operations environments of the participating agencies, we were collectively familiar with the diverse groups we'd be serving as well as their respective missions and work environments. So given who we were, and who we knew well, our success ultimately flowed from being able to conceptually place ourselves at *both ends of the contact channel* and then create what we'd want to experience there. And there lies the secret sauce of the CX culture! It's what I've come to call *enlightened creativity* -- the mental energy of the people closest to the customer who understand them best. Unleashing it is the true path to building and enhancing your customer's experience!

Our Roles, Challenges, and Opportunities

Together we play an unmatched strategic role as the face of government. We're the interface where the massive infrastructure of the world's largest service engine converges to deliver information and services across every line of business.[1] *Everyone*, including us, is a customer, stakeholder, and stockholder. Our external contact channels are the tip of the huge government iceberg that citizens see above the waterline. Our internal help desks and other support services drive efficiency in the unseen part of the iceberg, where they enhance the productivity of people and the effectiveness of systems that ultimately enable what we do. Altogether the combination of these should be envisioned as a huge ecosystem of service production and delivery which interconnects to serve the customer! This is how the leaders in CX across all sectors see their organization!

To outside thought leaders in the service field we're a quiet, complex, and poorly understood giant – highly diverse, dispersed yet ubiquitous, bureaucratic, and unfortunately very *disconnected* from each other. We tend to be much more tactical than strategic -- often distracted and crisis-driven by legislation and other mandates from politicians and budgeteers. Compared to our private sector counterparts we're seen as less focused on performance measurement (despite tons of rhetoric to the contrary), less receptive to risk or change, and too often hobbled by dispersed organizational decision making. The most visible drivers of our uniqueness are considered to be our unmatched *fiduciary responsibility* to those we serve and our complicated public sector *personnel systems.*

Not surprisingly, private sector "best practices" and service models are a poor fit for us *unless* they are first adapted to our unique role and restrictions. Yet far too often we try to blindly import them without first applying the modifications needed to make them effective in the public sector context. The main barrier to importing the customer relationship management ("*CRM*") paradigm into government was the driving premise of retaining data on a customer's past interactions to anticipate their personal preferences when dealing with them again. It sounded good until we rediscovered that people generally don't want government retaining individually identifiable data on them! In the case of CX, the driving premise of enhancing the brand of a given retailer versus competitors just doesn't apply! In our sector, there are almost never others who directly compete with what we do. Yet what our customers experience with any part of what they consider "government" is extrapolated as part of their collective impression to all the rest of us. This can be an inherent penalty to the image of those doing it best levied by those who aren't *yet* doing it so well and is unique to us!

We've been called the "Fortune 1" in part because everyone is our customer. While others often seek to stratify the customers they serve in order to be more responsive to their respective group needs, doing so presents a supreme challenge for us due to the ultimate size and complexity of our customer base. Citizens automatically and continually transfer to us their expectations based on their customer experiences in the private sector – an inherent demand that we continually evolve our services forward despite our many unique constraints. However, our "business case" to resource keeping up with what they expect is totally different than in the private sector where projected increases to revenue streams can be used to justify costs of improving services. We must usually instead persuade those who would fund us based on increased *cost efficiency* -- which does not correlate well with effectiveness in satisfying customers. In addition to these other challenges, many of us must also deliver services in inherently unpopular government lines of business such as taxation, enforcement, collections, and corrections, and/or to people who are dealing with traumatic life crises such as a death in the family or cancer.

Service technology is a whole separate and formidable challenge for us! Our acquisition processes are often so complex and cumbersome that many potential sources are essentially excluded. Far too many in our sector have been led astray by polished sales pitches, expensive system integrations, and empty promises of functionality after the sale from those that remain. Too often we tend to believe that the experts are those who have travelled farthest, hear what we want to hear in the sales process, and aren't equipped to ask enough insightful questions before we're stuck with something that doesn't work as promised in our unique environment. We're often pushed by politics to employ new technology for automated service delivery, but given that we must uniquely serve *everyone,* we find that our customers in some demographics are too locked into their channel preferences to make it comprehensively applicable. A key word of advice here: Whenever *you* consider or deal with service delivery systems, remember that *your* processes should not be governed by what's baked into a system by a vendor, but should instead be those that work most effectively for the constituents you serve based on *your* unique knowledge of their needs and preferences! If this can't be accommodated by a system you're considering, look elsewhere. Remember to "trust but verify" when buying. Much more on this later.

Amidst the challenges we face in meeting our collective

mission there are some tremendous opportunities as well.
The most promising of these is the potential power of
networking and benchmarking *within* government. Our
collective knowledge of government's customer and what
works for them is massive yet essentially unshared among
us. To capitalize on it, each of us must expand our focus
outward and reach out to our peers as a *key investment*
in doing our job better. We shouldn't be buying our
customer perspective from someone on the outside who
has nothing near the breadth of view that we together
have. We should instead invest the time to connect and
learn about delivering an excellent customer experience in
our sector from those who actually do it! We also need to
aggressively *market our mission* and increase our visibility
as *the* strategic function of government – continually
seeking creative ways to enhance awareness of how we
touch and enhance lives daily. We must also continually
take a fresh look through the eyes of our customer at what
we're doing! This requires us to *know them*, and each time
they touch us with needs or feedback should be seen as an
opportunity to better do so. Take full advantage of these
gifts! Customers, their expectations, service technology,
and service delivery practices continually evolve – and
so must we. Our mission, if done right, is truly a *journey*
which requires continuously watching for what's coming
over the horizon in order to keep *evolving forward* to meet
it. One of the most powerful resources for doing so is

your customer perspective at the front lines. Seek it out and use it!

* * *

[1] Lines of business in government service delivery are listed and defined in Appendix 1.

Finding Teams
Doing It Right

Early in my quest my peers within government were very
hard to find. As I visited various forums on service delivery
to share our team's lessons learned I would always try to
seek them out, but the results were usually slim because they
often weren't even there! Given our size and diversity, our
potential to learn together, grow professionally and synergize
to advance is practically limitless. The lost opportunities and
absence of bridges to the greater professional community
which I saw concerned me so much early on that I founded a
community of practice to foster networking and the sharing
of effective practices for service delivery that work in our
public sector environment. This subsequently became what
we know today as "Cgov."

One of the keystones of the Cgov outreach is the annual
Government Customer Service Excellence Awards program
which at this writing is in the eighteenth year. The driving
objective of this program has from the outset always been
to honor teams at all levels of government that effectively

apply what we'll see next as the foundations of CX culture to achieve substantiated high levels of customer and front line staff care. [2] A second but even more important objective has been to facilitate the sharing of their successful practices with their peers in government. Over many years these two objectives have been accomplished in partnership with established learning events as well as through our monthly electronic newsletter which today reaches a global audience of thousands at all levels of government. A more recently defined third objective is to draw upon the priceless archive of accumulated award nominations to describe the culture that delivers top CX in the public sector. The legacy of this objective may be the most enduring of all, serving as the primary resource for the principles, practices, and measures of CX culture shared here.

* * *

[2] Past winners of the Government Customer Service Excellence Awards through 2018 are listed in Appendix 2.

Foundations of
the Culture

Customers don't typically reach out to government instinctively. In fact, it's more often as a last resort -- preceded by procrastination, internet searches, asking friends, and/or any other avoidance mechanisms they think might work. And when they finally contact us, it's too often via the most costly contact channels – those directly involving people in real time -- which they instinctively envision as the shortest path to the *quick, accurate, courteous solution*.

The quick, accurate, courteous solution or *QACS* is the holy grail of both the customer in need *and* those who most effectively serve them. While the concept sounds deceivingly simple, delivering it consistently in a changing world to an evolving constituency with ever-escalating expectations in support of an evolving product or service requires a special kind of culture which is fully focused on both the providers and the receivers across all communication channels at all times. The complexity of this has been compared by one of us to "building the boat as we go down the river." Fully considered, it's an intimidating challenge!

Culture has been called the "group think of the people in it." As I looked back on our success, it soon became very clear that delivering the QACS was the group think that drove the high success of our contact services, and the culture we built around accomplishing it was our ultimate enabler. Upon further reflection, I identified the four foundational elements of this culture which I've since found to be intrinsic in the cultures of service providers elsewhere throughout government who excel in the experience they provide to their respective customer bases.

Teamwork is the first and most critical element in CX culture. The other pillars crumble unless it permeates the culture and cements everything together. Front line teams in this culture consistently identify and empathize with the customer, synergize as a way of life, and nimbly focus all of their resources as needed in real time. They proactively work together in an environment of trust and empowerment to quickly resolve customer issues and also ensure that all other members are ready to do so. However, in this environment where CX flourishes there's a much broader concept of teamwork which reaches from the front line team outward across the organization and sometimes beyond it. Later we'll explore practices from throughout government that make this happen.

Technical excellence, the second element, primarily reflects the organization's commitment to training, professionally developing, and career pathing of those responsible for creating and delivering the customer's experience. In our case, there was no room for technical error given that sometimes lives would be at stake. But enabled by a good budget and extended lead times to prepare due to program delays, we invested heavily in comprehensive initial front line training to ensure that our agents were fully prepared going out the gate to deliver the QACS. This investment proved so valuable in early results that we were subsequently resourced by the decision makers to continue it in order to stay on top of the rapid advances in science and technology which followed as the system matured. In the broader sense of CX culture, technical excellence also applies to your internal and customer processes as well as your applications of technology as we'll explore later.

Customer focus is the third element of the CX culture. It assures that all customers are treated with sincere empathy and courtesy at all times while their needs are being insightfully perceived and resolved. I like to call it the vital frosting on the service cake! Like the QACS it's a concept that sounds simple up front, but the full associated challenge is huge. The path to this one is truly *knowing* your customers, and you'll see later a wealth of practices used by those who excel in CX to do so.

The *solution concept* is the final foundational element. It simply means that the *initial* response to a customer's issue *fully resolves it without any further action required.* Driven by our vision, we were dedicated to doing things comprehensively right the first time. Public value has been defined as the combination of operational efficiency, constituent service levels, and political alignment. When constituents seek services from us, what we often *must* do for cost efficiency counters what they instinctively consider effective in meeting their needs. This is a challenge we share with the private sector, but in our case customer dissatisfaction can cause politicians to get involved which can be highly distracting and resource intensive for us. Across government, people who deliver services will quickly tell you that it is too expensive in terms of internal costs to try to resolve all customer issues during the initial contact. Experts, however, are in longstanding agreement that the total organizational costs of *not* doing so are much greater compared to doing it right the first time. And as you're no doubt aware as a customer yourself, the impact of true *first contact resolution* -- one of the key metrics of CX success – on customer satisfaction is tremendous. Focusing on the solution concept just drives it up!

To briefly summarize what we've covered so far, *the CX culture is one in which true teams apply their technical excellence in an environment of customer focus to achieve their shared vision of the QACS.* As we finish this brief introduction to the foundations of CX culture in government, you may wish to do a quick preliminary self-evaluation. If so, we suggest that you take a moment to consider objectively how well your team focuses on delivering the QACS by applying teamwork, technical excellence, customer focus, and the solution concept respectively. Then briefly capture your results for reference as we now explore how CX teams across government are doing it right!

At the Front Lines

Delivering an excellent customer experience is a *team sport*. If energy and effort are not freely and consistently invested in a shared vision of delivering the QACS by *all* of the people who have a role in doing so, quality CX just doesn't happen. It requires a special proactive self-improving culture to catch and fix glitches in service on the fly while also continually seeking ways to enhance the experience of the customer.

The imperative for teamwork in the CX culture begins at the front lines. Those who touch the customer across all channels, share a common quest to be prepared to fully resolve whatever the customer throws at them. They freely share their personal knowledge, skills, backgrounds, and abilities in real time and receive the same from their peers. They creatively expedite knowledge access for the rest of the team, and synergistically focus resources however needed to deliver the QACS at each customer's "moment of truth." In short, each of them is an *owner* doing whatever it takes to make the team's service delivery successful.

Training and professional development are a way of life in

CX culture where they are the uncontested top motivators and drivers of retention in both public and private sectors. In CX culture, training begins for new members well before they ever interact with customers. A comprehensive baseline training program which fully prepares new front line staff for launch sends the strongest possible message regarding the importance of what they will be doing, instills confidence in the team's vision, and assures consistency in the customer's experience. Regular team training is seen as a strong builder of cohesion because members learn and grow professionally *together* while interacting in the process. Mentoring is prolific and senior members are routinely paired with new ones as a resource to bring them fully up to speed in the work *and* the culture. Team members have living individual training plans which equip them with shared team knowledge and skills as well as those required to fulfill any specialties they are assigned. Training plans are developed and regularly updated in collaboration with those they guide, in order to enhance ownership and ensure thoroughness.

In our case, everyone on the team had one or more assigned specialty areas of responsibility which they *owned* on behalf of the team. This can be a huge motivator, but must be supported with regular time away from contact channels to fulfill. Experts concur that agents should be off channel a *minimum* of twenty percent of the time to mitigate the stress inherent in what we do and preclude burnout. Applied training and time to work on areas of specialty are *excellent* ways to invest it! Given that the ultimate beneficiary is the customer, the value potential of getting this one right is tremendous!

What's fundamental in the culture must be intrinsic in the performance management system for full success. In our case all individual performance plans specified use of *individual creativity* to identify ways to (1) make the team more effective, (2) enhance the assimilation and sharing of knowledge, (3) foster the team's professional growth and, of course, (4) continually improve the customer's experience. Performance plans such as this, and the evaluations conducted in support of them, actually *empower* team members by giving them license to apply their personal *creativity* and *customer perspective* to help evolve the team's customer care continually forward. As one award winner shared, "Our high level of customer service is sustainable because we have built our expectations into our internal culture and they are reinforced through our rewards and performance evaluation system."

Learning events, membership in professional organizations, and external certifications related to service delivery present great opportunities to foster professional growth and reinforce ownership in front liners. Members who represent your team in these outside activities should always do so with the inherent charter to share their learning with the rest of the team afterward. Career pathing should be a topic touched upon by every performance discussion as part of your professional development program. In our case, the investment in team member training was never considered "lost" in the bigger picture of the organization when people moved to other areas. Rather, they became highly trained assets in other specialties who fully understood our mission and often served as our resources and advocates there. It should be noted that, although it gave them tremendous professional pride to know they were in high demand elsewhere, most of our members stayed with us over time because they liked our culture and believed strongly in the value of what they were doing – a priceless benefit of having the right culture!

A pervasive sense of *ownership* is fundamental in CX culture and it's fascinating to see the various ways those who succeed cultivate it. Those shared in nominations include peer quality monitoring, peer awards, internal quality management groups, a team role in developing and updating policy and procedures, growing internal experts in key specialties, and assigned responsibility for specialized supporting functions such as library, knowledge base, and technology. In some teams, members are assigned responsibility for public relations outreach. Among my favorite related practices shared by others is requiring new applicants to sign a pledge

cost is small or none, and the dividends are large in making CX happen.

How can you monitor the health of your team culture at the front lines? Number one is probably the least frequently used across government -- a regular and carefully constructed, administered, and analyzed *employee satisfaction survey*. Studies show that the results of these are usually highly correlated with your customers' satisfaction. As a friend says insightfully, "Happy workers create happy customers." Look also at attrition – who's leaving and why. Usually it should be low. However, a high rate is not necessarily out of line if you're training well, career-pathing people, and have a stressful mission. Keep in mind that new people coming in behind those who leave have fresh perspective on what you do, and evaluate their first impressions carefully -- especially if they were previously your customers. First contact resolution can help you infer how well people are working together. Some who excel at CX go a step further and regularly observe and evaluate specifically how well agents work together in handling especially difficult or complex customer issues. The frequency of suggestions received from the front lines illustrates how much they think their input is valued – it reflects their sense of ownership and it should be high. Finally, knowledge base additions and updates reflect how well invested people are in empowering each other with one of your most key resources. For all of these indicators, the trends over time are at least as important as the values themselves.

* * *

[3] *Government Customer Service Days* are celebrated by service teams at all levels of government during the first consecutive Tuesday through Thursday period of December each year. For details and celebration ideas, email *daryl@cgovcop.org*.

Building Bridges

In true CX culture we take the initiative to build bridges to the groups elsewhere in our own organization which have responsibility to define, develop, administer, modify, and update the programs, services, etc. which we support. The bridges we build enable us to reach into the organization at the moment of truth to meet the needs and expectations of our customer.

These are documented as *operating level agreements* or *OLAs* and must be built upon mutual trust and respect. They enable us to interact productively and efficiently with other teams on behalf of the organization's customers. To be effective, OLAs must be binding, unambiguous, regularly reviewed on behalf of both teams (including compliance and performance data), and kept current in the ever-changing world of CX. They're not easy to build and maintain but, if done right, they offer huge dividends in delivering the QACS -- especially for the most complex customer issues.

The bridge building begins with -- no surprise -- *people.* We must reach across internal silos, beginning with *two-way internal marketing* to make the other groups aware of what we do on behalf of the organization and also to learn -- from their perspective -- what they do. From our end, it's all about making the case for their help when needed to take care of the organization's customer while gaining genuine empathy for their competing priorities in providing it. The conversation is not always easy. It can involve management personalities, turfs, organizational politics, resource allocation, and much more that is complex in nature. Our case is best made using what a friend calls the "*value proposition*" which is simply *explaining what's in it for them*. In our case, using examples and data from our tracking systems, we demonstrated how the knowledge they shared with us was carefully captured and re-used many times to resolve repetitive customer issues without their further involvement. We also persuaded them to grant us access to internal experts in real time under specifically defined conditions with the value proposition of eliminating internal paperwork and saving their team time.

Each OLA requires ongoing care and maintenance as managers, programs, and much more invariably change over time. The top CX teams often assign specific members to interface, update agreements, and generally maintain good relations with other internal departments – a great opportunity for individual ownership and professional development. Exchange of personnel is also a great way to ensure ongoing connection and understanding between groups. In our case, baseline training for new members included visiting our enterprise partners and meeting the people there. Joint team meetings are an excellent way to accomplish the regular reviews of OLAs -- especially if you provide snacks! Be alert for common training needs between teams and use them as an opportunity to bring personnel together to learn while getting better acquainted in the same classroom! It's *very* important to freely acknowledge the other teams – especially in front of management -- for helping you care for customers. In our case, when we received a major award in a very special ceremony, we in turn presented awards of appreciation at the same time to each of our enterprise partners for their respective roles in our success. In summary, seek and seize opportunities of all types to get and keep the members of yours and the other teams familiar with each other.

Well done OLAs can positively impact your technical excellence in a big way. Related practices shared by CX leaders include regular technical exchange meetings between teams, automated tracking of customer issues across the enterprise, sharing knowledge bases, subject matter experts providing special training to front line agents, creating reference directories of experts by specialty in the organization, cross-training between groups, and partnering to incorporate customer-based perspective into program design and changes. The latter maximizes your strategic value and impact in the organization. Your customer perspective and OLA performance data can also have high value in budgeting to serve the organization's customers. Share them with management!

Let's look at indicators to monitor how well you're teaming with your enterprise partners. OLA compliance is a great place to start. How well other teams honor their agreements with you reflect how well you've marketed the organizational importance of what you do and delivered a viable value proposition to them. Adherence to the OLA review process also shows how these relationships are valued in the midst of competing priorities. Look carefully at how frequently customer issues must be elevated elsewhere to be resolved and work with the other teams involved to acquire the additional knowledge to handle the most common ones internally. Look also at the time required to resolve your customer issues involving other teams to gauge their internal prioritization of meeting your needs.

In the case of external partner teams, we must reach farther and it's often a little more complex because they are in a different management chain, different level of government, or even outside government. Regardless, the process still involves the bridging concepts we just covered for enterprise partners. Examples of this scenario from nominations include interagency collaboration to provide complex training for foreign trade specialists, city governments teaming with charitable organizations that provide social services, partnering with media to jointly inform the public during emergencies, and sharing of service delivery resources between organizations during emergencies and disasters. Related practices shared in our nominations include offering misdirect services to the correct phone number or URL and partner agencies working together to establish the infrastructure to directly transfer calls between them. Many web portals, notably at the state level, have working agreements to redirect those who could not find what they needed to libraries for research.

The prime health indicators for these partnerships are essentially the same as for internal partners. The bottom line objective is an ongoing evaluation of how well your external partners like and honor the relationship and -- most important -- how it is affecting your customer. In this tier of teaming, the field of stakeholders broadens and your sources of feedback must also. Key indices shared by other CX teams include referral rates, external call transfer rates, OLA compliance metrics, and effectiveness of OLA reviews and feedback between the teams. Success in reaching externally for help in serving your customers requires, as shared by one team, *"fostering collaboration, communication, and trust."* In fact, this concept should be routinely applied more broadly to *all* of your team building efforts in support of making great CX happen!

Teaming with Knowledge

Whenever we touch on the topic of technical excellence, many of us instantly jump to thoughts of systems and technology. These can be great enablers, and in some respects the government service delivery world today is obsessed with them – especially as potential drivers in lowering costs. But the definition of technical excellence in a quality CX culture is much broader and doesn't even begin there. It starts with (no surprise) *people*.

As we've already seen, training must be a way of life and professional growth continuous in a high performance CX culture. Central to this is the comprehensive valuing and sharing of knowledge and making it immediately findable for the rest of the team. If we don't know something, we have to be able to find it quickly to achieve the QACS. In the most basic terms, what we deliver to the customer is *our knowledge packaged in our culture*.

One CX team cited their regular "Stump the Kbase

Contest" which challenges members to identify needs and incorporate new entries which fulfill them into their knowledge base. Others cited addressing knowledge base contributions in performance appraisals to reinforce the concept. More practices related to team technical excellence shared in nominations include delivering user training (a great way to assure customer knowledge *and* know customers better), assuring information consistency across channels, protecting sensitive personal information while also providing easy personal access, conducting periodic specialized training on the top ten customer issue types, skill-based routing of customer issues to internal experts, and implementation of a cross-departmental shared knowledge base. Above all, those who do CX best continuously seek ways to maximize the value of the team members' diverse interests and backgrounds in caring for customers by applying their collective enlightened creativity.

First contact resolution or "*FCR*" is a great primary indicator of your team's technical excellence. *But* the term should be strictly defined as in the glossary for this measure to be meaningful. I've actually seen teams tweak their definition of FCR just to make their performance look good! That in the end result does no good for either them or their customer. The volume and accuracy of knowledge base updates are also good indicators. Watch your accuracy scores from quality control monitoring and the percentage of customer issues requiring assistance from other teams to resolve. Finally, keep an eye on employee satisfaction scores. Technical excellence drives readiness to respond which is a proven prime motivator of those who excel at delivering a positive experience to your customer.

Processes Are Big

Most of us don't immediately consider processes a key
component of technical excellence. It's not intuitive until
after you've read the first few hundred award nominations and
seen how the best teams focus on maximizing the customer-
friendliness of their internal and customer processes! Your
processes for access, queuing, prioritizing, delivering service
continuity across channels, elevation, quality control,
evaluation and much more play a huge role in defining the
customer's experience. In fact, *how* something is resolved is
sometimes much more memorable to the customer afterward
than the solution itself! Like OLAs, processes must be fully
documented, binding, unambiguous, and regularly reviewed
– always with enlightened focus on *your customer* -- to be
effective. One of my favorite ways to illustrate the impact of
processes on your customer's experience is to challenge you
to *put yourself in your own queue*. Literally! Anonymously
call or text or co-browse on the web site or touch the team
for service through other channels to see how your customers
really feel treated. Do this regularly across varied contact
channels, evaluate what you experience objectively, and apply
your results continuously.

Notable processes shared in nominations include regular problem trending and root cause analysis for customer issues, applying feedback from live channels to improve web services, offering the live person option across channels, delivering on-line customer forums, training customers on line to use web self-service, converting the web site to red alert status during emergencies, publishing a newsletter to keep customers aware of online services, and posting downloadable forms to save time for walk-in customers.

The *best* guidance I can offer for ensuring customer-friendly processes is in a previous book which captures the results from over fifty experienced government service managers representing diverse lines of business who put themselves in the customer's shoes to envision and capture what they would want as citizens given what they knew as service professionals. I think you'll find it valuable in designing the processes your customers *want* to experience! [4]

* * *

[4] *Government Customer Service Standards* is available by emailing *daryl@cgovcop.org*.

Technology Done Right

Service technology is our enabler. Properly applied, it facilitates the fast capture, access, application, tracking, and research of massive amounts of information that makes what we do as effective as possible for the *customer* and as efficient as possible for *us*. And it all begins with the acquisition process.

Years ago when I was asked to do an article on selecting service technology my immediate response was "no." But after further considering all the *wrong* moves I'd seen, I decided to share what I'd learned from them. And it's all still just as valid as it was then. First is to seek others performing similar functions with the same or similar systems to what you're considering. If you don't have the reach for this, insist that any vendor you're considering point you to others of their government customers who fit, and then visit them *without* the vendor present to discuss their experience and satisfaction. Be sure to cover integration with existing systems and support (including cost) after the sale. Second, seize opportunities such as conference trade shows (usually free to attend) to see side-by-side demonstrations of systems and ask incisive questions. Pose the same questions to each vendor you're considering and carefully compare and freely ask them to clarify their answers. Third, explore during the selection process what's involved to acquire the internal expertise to administer the new system, including user modifications, reports, and basic changes in functionality. As part of this, examine their annual maintenance agreement and find out exactly what is provided in return for the associated cost. Fourth and finally, as already mentioned, *verify* that the system can incorporate and accommodate *your* customer processes. Don't become a slave to your new system (or vendor)!

Our case was somewhat unique with respect to service technology. We were fortunate to find a good basic product for our primary tracking system that was being fielded around the time we launched, and we grew together with the vendor and the capabilities of their system for many years with great success. We invested substantially up front to ensure that we could fully administer the system and even grew an internal expert for that purpose. That person became so proficient that, over time, the company would ask us to evaluate their proposed enhancements and get our ideas for new or improved functionality. As part of the latter we did a continual market watch to keep track of what was out there and stay aware of how our system compared. The training investment up front paid handsomely in terms of their responsiveness to our needs as we and their system evolved – pretty hard to get at any price! Over the years we acquired other ancillary products from the same vendor with similar success, largely due to our rather unique level of internal expertise.

Some creative and responsive applications of technology shared in nominations include automated call transfers to other agencies, automated cell phone notifications to constituents by geographic area, tracking of customer information across contact channels, automated ticket status updates sent to customers, automated service level alerts sent to the team, enabling customers to submit issues on line, automatically transferring voice data between different IVR applications to eliminate repeating, and easy font size adjustment for seniors and the vision-impaired. One of *my* favorites unites GPS technology with the web to empower citizens to track snow plows on line during winter weather emergencies! And one of the greatest customer pleasers shared is *automatic* transfer of contact records when a contact is transferred internally!

Measures of your success in processes and applying technology include both customer and staff satisfaction. If they think your automated processes need to be better, it will definitely show. Watch, of course, for any feedback on the processes themselves and follow up. Keep an eye also on self-service utilization rates as an indicator of how well your "Level 0" system is working for customers. Technology helps to drive resolution times which should be watched as well. As indicators of how well technology is working internally, watch knowledge base utilization measures and especially the effectiveness of your *taxonomy system* for classifying customer issues into categories. The latter can have massive adverse impact on searches if it's not intuitive to agents and others who research your records – especially in real time to respond to customers. It should be regularly reviewed and updated in a timely manner whenever needed.

Our level of technical excellence is inherently reflected in everything we do. Like teamwork it must be continuously cultivated and applied to the specific needs of our customer. We hope what's been shared here will help you do so!

The Quest to Know Customers

In CX culture, we share a continuous quest to know our customers and their needs better. Some call government's customers "captives" because we're often the only source of what they need. But in this culture we always strive to treat customers in a manner that would *earn their business* regardless. As a key part of doing so, we prize *all* of their feedback – especially complaints -- and carefully apply it to evolve their experience continuously forward.

The value of customer feedback can't be overemphasized. We must continuously seek new and creative ways to acquire it without imposing on those who hesitate to invest their time to provide it to us. Complaints are great! However, studies have shown that very few customers will actually expend the effort to complain. More often they will instead tell others about what they see as a bad experience. The few who complain directly should be emphatically thanked for sharing their perspective and assured that what they provide will be analyzed carefully from their perspective with an eye to improvement. Making your complaint process as visible and user-friendly as possible can enhance how much of this valuable feedback type you get. Absence of complaints doesn't mean you're doing a good job if they don't know how to complain! Objectively chosen focus groups are a great resource because they are made up of customers who have already agreed in advance to provide input to help us improve. As our team discovered, there is massive value in having a free form field on customer surveys so that those who wish to do so can go into detail. You'll be amazed at what you can catch there if you read carefully! In our case, returned customer surveys were shared with everyone on the team so that we could see and act as a team on our status in the eyes of the customer and our opportunities to improve.

As we completed preparations to launch our contact center, we invited representatives from agency headquarters worldwide to a meticulous review of our operations plan on behalf of their field sites. Their primary concerns centered on the *continuity* of the experience – especially points of vulnerability like queueing, transfers, hold, and tracking. As we later learned, *all* customers *instinctively* fear and dislike *waiting*, *having to start over*, and *repeating information*. The best teams alleviate this in real time by such methods as providing tracking numbers, capturing callback information, replacing silence on hold with recordings, estimating wait time and offering the option to instead be contacted, and automatically transferring contact records when the contact is transferred. Our future customers were also concerned about how we would prioritize issues for resolution in real time. They were very happy to learn that it would be driven by the impact of the associated issue on the site's ability to accomplish their respective mission based on published guidelines. Other CX teams have shared that they *always* prioritize issues, and decide when they are resolved, *jointly* with the customer.

Seasons of change are often when the customer needs us most and when we accordingly have to be the most resourceful to respond to bumps in the road. Progressive teams supporting technology employ staggered roll-outs to better balance customer needs for assistance with the resources available to provide it. The same can be applied to program changes as well. Another team created a temporary support group to assist users of a new web assistance portal -- a great way to foster the customer's move to a more efficient channel! Many of us experience a seasonality of workload, such as for the IRS during tax season, and plan ahead to project demand and augment staffing during those periods. The same can be applied to predictable changes such as program updates and additions.

Some other practices and perspectives shared by CX teams include customer-intuitive access to posted information

with no need to know the organization's division of
responsibilities. Many teams design and deliver customer
training to enhance customer knowledge and also get to
know them better. Overlapping shifts to assure continuity
of handling and expanding hours of operation to meet
customer needs came up repeatedly. Aligning OLAs with
posted customer service levels helps to assure that these
important customer agreements can always be met. Some
use geographic IP data to respond to online inquiries
with localized information. True to the QACS concept,
many pride themselves on their driving vision of one-stop
comprehensive assistance. Finally, two practices shared that I
found refreshingly unique were spontaneously asking phone
customers if they are satisfied with the pace of the call and
creating a "mobile branch" that travels to provide public
services on site in remote areas.

The key measure to follow in tracking the success of your
customer focus is, of course, customer satisfaction. It should
be one of your most key metrics and trends in it should be
closely watched. But there are other types of feedback that
can help fill out the picture. In our case, our customers were
sometimes under extreme operational pressures to protect
lives and their demeanor reflected it when they contacted
us. Some of these customers actually got back with us later
to apologize. This I consider one of the most meaningful
reflections of their high respect and trust for us. Perhaps

even more meaningful than any metric! Customers *love* first contact resolution and you can use that measure to see in part how often you're delighting them. Look also at wait times in queue and time to resolve to see how you're impacting what they consider their most valued resource. *Everyone* who touches government for help is in a hurry. They hate waiting on hold, slow response web pages, being queued for chat responses, and everything else that takes any of their time, so strive to be respectful of it however you process their contacts. Also consider convening regular focus groups of customers and listening carefully to them as a way to continuously evolve your customer's experience forward. Finally, consider the advice shared earlier to *put yourself in your own queue*!

The Destination

True CX culture in government gives us the magic mix of
empowered creativity and customer understanding which
delivers a customer experience that is fully empathetic,
totally responsive, and always *evolving forward*. This culture
provides the right human touch for each human being in
need of our help, and our signature product is our knowledge
packaged in it. Smartly administered automation enables
us to deliver our trademark *quick, accurate, courteous solution*
via the customer's preferred channel – always from the
perspective of *people helping people.*

Within our organization we are the hub of the service
ecosystem. We skillfully establish and maintain bridges
of understanding built on mutual trust which enable us to
readily work with our enterprise partners whenever needed
on behalf of our customers. Externally, we're seen and serve
as the helping hand of our organization for those in need.
Our unique understanding of the organization's customers
is our greatest strategic asset, and we seek continuously to
improve our application of it to delivering the experience
they want. As the greater face of government we are the

customer touchpoint for the most massive service machine on earth. Every time we deliver a great experience, we grow trust in government by fulfilling with excellence the most basic function it performs.

We are each proud of our team, our culture, our partnerships, our organizational value, and our greater role in government. Our greatest pride, however, is in the high quality experience which all of these together enable us to deliver to our customer. This is the focus of our *shared vision*!

The Journey Goes On

The culture we've attempted to define here is in a way like the ancient pyramids. Many experts have tried for a long time to figure out how they were built, yet the picture is *still* not complete. The pyramids were finished long ago, however, but this culture won't ever be completed! In fact, the bar rises *daily* as empowered teams in existing pockets of CX culture throughout government continue to creatively contemplate and then enhance the experience of those they serve because *they want to*. These progressive practice leaders make CX culture a *living* paradigm which self-improves over time as customer needs and expectations continuously evolve. And this is perhaps our culture's most distinguishing trait as well as the source of a term we've been using here which we believe captures the essence of it. As you strive to always deliver the most responsive possible experience to your customer, may you, and the experience you deliver to them, always *evolve forward*.

"Boldly go where customer service has never gone before."

-- A GCSEA winning team

APPENDIX ONE

LINES OF BUSINESS IN GOVERNMENT SERVICE DELIVERY

Shared by Mr. Robert Smudde

1. **Information**
Transfer of information between government and customer.

2. **Benefits**
Payments and/or services that accrue to customers.

3. **Duty**
Interactions which are required of customers.

4. **Commercial**
Specific services or items for which customers directly pay government.

5. **Intergovernmental**
Interactions among government, law enforcement, and/or military organizations.

6. Emergency

Response to destruction or imminent threat to life and/or property.

7. Other

Interactions not included in any of the other six types above.

APPENDIX TWO

WINNERS OF THE GOVERNMENT CUSTOMER SERVICE EXCELLENCE AWARDS

2002

Social Security Administration Network Customer Service
Center *

Kansas Department of Human Resources **

Department of Education Help Desk ***

Navy Defense Messaging System Consolidated Help Desk ****

Army IMCEN Help Desk *****

2003

Department of Commerce Trade Information Center *

National Weather Service Network Control Center **

Hampton, VA 311 Customer Call Center ***

General Services Administration National Contact Center ****

2004

Department of Education Information Resource Center *

District of Columbia Web Portal **
Township of Franklin, NJ ***
Veterans' Administration Insurance Center Call Center ****

2005
Social Security Administration Chicago Region
   Management and Operations Support Branch *
NASA Information Support Center **
Utah.gov ***
Department of Labor National Contact Center ****

2006
Space and Naval Warfare Systems Center, New Orleans *
Utah.gov **
Miami-Dade 311 Answer Center ***
Space and Naval Warfare Systems Center, New Orleans ****

2007
IRS Employee Resource Center *
Military Health System Network Operations Center **
Navy Global Distance Support Center ***
Connecticut Business Response Center ****

2008
New Hampshire IT Help Desk Services *
Navy Defense Messaging System Consolidated Help Desk **
Undersea Warfare Center Keyport Navy Marine Corps
   Intranet Transition Team ***

EPA Call Center ****

2009

Small Business Administration Disaster Assistance
    Customer Service Center *
City of Irving, TX IT Service Division **
Martin County, FL IT Service Desk ***
Small Business Administration Disaster Assistance
    Customer Service Center ****

2010

U. S. Patent and Trademark Office Facilities Help Desk *
Utah.gov **
U. S. Geological Survey Service Desk ***
U. S. Geological Survey Service Desk ****

2011

Ohio Administrative Services Financials Program
    Management Office *
NASA Shared Services Center Customer Contact Center **
National Women's Health Information Center ***
IRS Travel Services Branch ****

2012

City of Jacksonville, FL 630CITY *
Army Medical Department Enterprise Service Desk **
Veterans' Administration Insurance Customer Service
    Center ***

Veterans' Administration Insurance Customer Service
   Center ****

2013

Defense Imagery Management Operations Center *
U. S. Geological Survey Service Desk **
Department of Agriculture MyPlate and SuperTracker
   Customer Support Center ***
Department of Agriculture Forest Service Customer Help
   Desk ****

2014

IRS Payroll/Personnel Systems *
District of Columbia Public Safety **
Customs and Immigration Service International Operations
   Division ***
District of Columbia Public Safety ****

2015

Richland County, SC Development Services *
IRS Debt Management Implementation Team **
Defense Logistics Agency Customer Interaction Center ***
Richland County, SC Development Services ****

2016

District of Columbia Public Safety *
U. S. Geological Survey Service Desk **

National Science Foundation IT Central Help Services ***
District of Columbia Public Safety ****

2017

Federal Aviation Administration Logistics Center Customer
    Service Branch *
Veterans' Administration Insurance Center **
National Archives and Records Administration History
    Hub ***
NASA Shared Services Center Enterprise Service Desk ****

2018

Knoxville, TN 3-1-1 Center for Service Innovation *
City of Centennial, CO Survey Platform Transition and
    Implementation of Satisfaction Alerts **
Defense Imagery Management Operations Center ***
Small Business Administration Disaster Assistance
    Customer Service Center ****

*	Teamwork Excellence Winner
**	Technical Excellence Winner
***	Customer Focus Excellence Winner
****	Overall Excellence Winner
*****	Special award for heroism and dedication to customers in the aftermath of the terrorist attacks on 9/11/2001

ACRONYMS

Cgov
Government Customer Service Community of Practice

Cgov eNews
Monthly electronic newsletter published by Cgov

CRM
Customer Relationship Management

CX
Customer Experience

OLA
Operating level agreement

QACS
Quick, accurate, courteous solution

SLA
Service level agreement

GLOSSARY

Best practices
Loosely used term that ignores the complexity of transferring practices in the public sector. Often employed in an attempt to impress by those who don't have another basis for doing so.

Customer experience
The summary impression resulting from all interactions (both direct and indirect) with the source of a product or service.

Customer experience culture
Organizational service paradigm in which true teams apply technical excellence in an environment of customer focus to achieve their shared vision of consistently delivering a quick, accurate, courteous solution to customers in need.

Enlightened creativity
The mental energy of the people closest to the customer who understand them best.

Enterprise partners
Other teams within the same organization upon which a service team is dependent for knowledge and support in serving their customers.

First contact
The *initial* exchange of information between organization and customer regarding a specific customer issue.

Government Customer Service Community of Practice
Professional organization founded to foster networking and exchange of effective practices among people who direct, manage, and deliver government services. Also known as "*C*gov."

Operating level agreement
Standards for the timeliness and responsiveness of support to a service team from their enterprise and external partners.

Quick, accurate, courteous solution
The comprehensive response to a customer issue which is the shared vision of high performance customer experience teams.

Queue
Customers who have connected with one of the organization's service channels and are awaiting service at a given time.

Service level agreement

Standards for the timeliness and responsiveness of service to a customer from a service team.

MEET THE AUTHOR

Daryl Covey is a longstanding advocate for effective service delivery in government. His passion is facilitating the sharing of effective service practices and fostering effective service culture in the public sector. He is the founder and facilitator of the *Government Customer Service Community of Practice* ("*C*gov"), editor of the monthly *C*gov *e*News, author of *Government Customer Service Standards*, and creator of the annual *Government Customer Service Excellence Awards* and *Government Customer Service Days*.

For many years Daryl has served variously as chair, panelist, facilitator, advisor, speaker, instructor, and consultant on effective service delivery for a wide variety of events, forums, and organizations. He is retired from federal service which included more than twenty years building, managing, and sharing lessons learned from high impact service delivery which was recognized with a wealth of awards for excellence. In retirement he serves as a local elected official. You can email him at *daryl@cgovcop.org*.

ABOUT CGOV

The *Government Customer Service Community of Practice* ("*C*gov") facilitates networking and the sharing of effective practices among the special people who direct, manage, and deliver the services of government. This outreach originated in the early 1990s and today enjoys global participation spanning all lines of business at all levels of government. Participation is free and open to all government employees. Subscriptions, sponsorships, and partnerships are available to all others. You can learn more about *C*gov by emailing *daryl@cgovcop.org*.

www.ingramcontent.com/pod-product-compliance
Lightning Source LLC
Chambersburg PA
CBHW061159180526
45170CB00002B/875